VActors:
Virtual Actors
on the Screen

by Annette Pry

PEARSON

Glenview, Illinois • Boston, Massachusetts • Chandler, Arizona
Upper Saddle River, New Jersey

Can a dinosaur walk down a city street? Can a cartoon mouse talk with a person? Can people fight with dragons? Do such things happen in real life?

No, they don't. But they can look like they happen with computer animation. We see impossible things in our video games, on television, and in the movies. Human actors and actors made by computers now appear in the same movies together. Actors made by computers are called "virtual actors."

---

cartoon: a drawing, usually funny
animation: making something look like it is moving
virtual: made to look real, or almost real

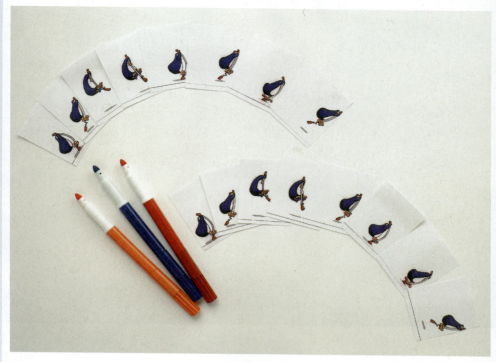

It takes many drawings such as these to make cartoon characters appear to move.

    Before we had movies, artists made pictures that appeared to move. Artists would draw many pictures of an animal or person. Each picture was slightly different. These drawings were shown one after the other. If the drawings were shown very fast, the animal or the person appeared to move.

    This process is called *animation*—making still pictures appear to move. Animation is used to make cartoon characters walk, talk, dance, and sing on television and in movies.

---

still: not moving

In the 1930s, people made long movies using animated characters. They used thousands of drawings. Princesses, horses, rabbits, and talking birds all appeared in these cartoon movies.

Today, we still have cartoon characters in movies, but artists don't have to draw by hand. They use computers to produce, or make, many drawings in seconds. With the help of computers, artists make the characters seem to move. Computers have changed the way cartoons and movies are made.

Computers can store lots of information. Artists can use this information to create characters. The artists decide many things about the characters. They decide how the characters will look, move, smile, and frown. Artists use computers to bring these characters to life.

This new kind of character is called a *virtual actor*, or a *VActor*. A virtual actor is the image of an actor or character that a computer creates. The VActor appears on a computer screen, a television, or in a movie. It looks like it is alive. It can move, talk, smile, or fly. Virtual actors can do almost anything that people do. But remember, VActors are really just pictures that appear to move.

Artists must also create a background for their VActors. Will the VActors walk through cities? Will they do battle in space? Will they swim in a landscape with rivers or lakes? Artists use computers to create a virtual world for their virtual actors. Some movies with real actors also use virtual backgrounds.

Artists can use computers to create backgrounds and landscapes for a movie.

Images of people created on a computer.

People have already seen many VActors in movies and video games. We have seen virtual dinosaurs that look like they are really alive. You can play a video game with one of your favorite sports stars.

VActors are very entertaining, but will we ever be able to replace real people in movies with VActors? Will computers ever be able to create virtual people who look and act exactly like real people?

---

entertaining: fun to watch or play with; amusing

So far, computers have not created a perfect VActor face. That face must be able to show happiness, sadness, worry, and joy. It must have lines and wrinkles. It must change and move hundreds of times each minute.

We now have VActors that look like dinosaurs, robots, and animals. But making a VActor that looks like a real person is much harder. People know when a face in a movie is real or virtual. And people like to watch real faces!

But computers are getting more powerful all the time. VActors are getting more and more realistic. One day soon, you might be asking, "Is it real or virtual?"